A Conversation Guide for

●

A Language of Healing for a Polarized Nation

●

Creating safe environments for
conversations about race, politics,
sexuality, and religion

By
Wayne Jacobsen, Arnita Willis Taylor,
and Robert L. Prater

International Standard Book Number
978-1-7340153-5-5

Blue Sheep Media
BlueSheepMedia.com
2902 East C Street | Torrington, WY 82240
p. 201.240.7106 | 213.408.9322
email: publish@bluesheepmedia.com

Cover and Interior designs: Charles Brock, www.brockbookdesignco.com

Printed in the United States of America
Original Printing August 2020

CONTENTS

"It doesn't matter if the group is a church or a gang or a sewing circle or masculinity itself, asking members to dislike, disown, or distance themselves from another group of people as a condition of 'belonging' is always about control and power. I think we have to question the intentions of any group that insists on disdain toward other people as a membership requirement."

— Brené Brown, in *Daring Greatly*

INTRODUCTION

We are thrilled that you have chosen to dive deeper into conversations with others relating to our book, *A Language of Healing for a Polarized Nation*. We understand not everyone will be on board for this in a group environment, particularly given the subject matter, but we believe these conversations are important. It is pivotal that each person in your group reads the designated chapter and give some thought to the action points *prior* to the meeting time. Individual preparation leads to a richer group discussion experience.

Our goal is for this workbook to be completed in a small group format. We recommend keeping your group size to fewer than ten participants. One reason for a smaller number is the nature of the material. Another reason is to give adequate time for each member to discuss and share with thought and ease. The recommended time is sixty to ninety minutes. The first part of the discussion guide directly relates to the individual as they identify their main points to remember. This section is followed by the group part of the discussion guide.

If you are initiating the formation of the group, be careful not to become a "talking head" or "instructor." Your role as a facilitator is to promote discussion by using the questions provided. Don't feel the need to use all of them but choose the ones most appropriate and helpful for your group. Intentionally invite all voices into the discussion. In addition, keep the group discussion time focused on the book context and not outside issues that arise. Please understand you have permission to process the workbook as it benefits your unique group mix. In some meetings, you may cover all the points; other meetings, maybe only a few.

If your intent is to use this for a midsize gathering, break the large group into smaller subgroups of five to seven people. Again, conversation is the goal of this guide. As a result, lead with a lot of open-ended questions. We have provided a complimentary list of conversation starters and questions on the website, www.alanguageofhealing.com.

Now, go forth and understand others!

If you want some ideas about how to facilitate your group, please see Appendix 1: Facilitation Tips on page 88.

If your group has previous relationships (church, neighborhood, or friendships) or is planning to meet during a number of weeks, you might find these group activities will broaden your experience. See Appendix 2: Team-Building Exercises on page 91.

"You can safely assume you've created God in your own image when it turns out that God hates all the same people you do."

— Anne Lamott

SECTION 1

An Opportune Moment

The country appears hopelessly polarized by media and political parties. Fortunately, there are only a few people who profit from the divisive climate of our nation. There are an increasing number of people who are tired of the paralysis of government and the rancor of the dialogue.

There has never been a better time for us to learn how to communicate more effectively with the people in our lives, especially those with whom we have significant disagreements. It will revitalize old friendships and open doors to new ones. We don't have to agree with each other to explore better avenues of mutual respect and cooperation.

1

A Fork in the Road

Are you tired of all the animosity in our national dialogue? Are you sick of every mention of religion or politics among family and friends that leaves you divided and angry? Have you had enough of social media exchanges that divide us into two hostile camps on every issue, with each side's proposed solution so completely exaggerated as to be unrealistic?

We hope you are. So are we! We are three regular Americans who are convinced that our current course is not only paralyzing our national dialogue, but also destroying our social fabric. We're looking for others who want to change the conversation from the rhetoric of polarization to a language of healing, where honest differences don't have to destroy relationships and where we can find common ground through mutual respect and compassion.

Before You Arrive

The individual part of the conversation guide is for your personal exploration and discovery of thoughts. You may or may not choose to share these with the open group.

After reading chapter one, take several minutes to ponder the following thoughts and questions:

1. Think back to a specific conversation where disagreement led to hard feelings. Would a different approach have led to a more peaceful outcome?

2. If you have ever learned a foreign language, remember the process. How long did it take to develop a basic understanding? How long did it take to become fluent?

3. Were you able to recognize yourself in the chapter? Were you the majority voice or the minority voice?

Let the Conversation Begin

(Note: Be empowered to use as many or as few of these questions for your conversation time. Customize the use to your specific group.)

Break into groups of three or four and discuss the following:

1. How much time have you spent around people who are not like you? How important is proximity when breaking down barriers?

2. Do you think it's possible to have respect for someone
   with whom you disagree?

3. How do empathy and understanding factor in to
   learning a language of healing?

Learning

1. How familiar were you with the difference between
   compromise and *consensus*?

2. Think of a time when you respected someone without
   agreeing with them. Have you ever experienced a lack
   of agreement leading to a lack of respect?

3. Are you able to recall a time when simply spending
   time with someone changed your views? Recall both a
   positive and a negative change.

Action: What Will You Do Differently?

At the end of this chapter the authors offered three possible actions to help you implement a strategy for change. At
this part of the process, consider taking an opportunity to
reflective journal through each of the action points. As in

any good reflection exercise, take time to pause and thoughtfully turn the new information you have gained into intentional personal insight.

Crawl: *As you stand at your "fork in the road," what would most inspire you to learn the language of healing?*

Walk: *Can you think of someone you could invite to learn it with you, so you can practice with each other?*

Run: *Schedule a coffee or lunch with one person who is very different from you, that you would like to know better.*

Share

As you begin your journey to learn a new language of healing, find a partner to learn alongside. Along the way, spend time comparing notes and sharing stories of your progress. As you become more proficient, reach out and invite others to join you.

2

What's in It for Me?

---○---

It's difficult to buck the status quo. Even if it isn't all that you hope for, it is at least predictable and you already know how to navigate it. Anything new, especially without guarantees, is always a risk. Learning the language of healing requires the courage to face the unknown and the willingness to go against the flow. And yet, some of our most impactful experiences come when we push beyond the status quo despite our reluctance.

Learning a new way to communicate with people around you, especially those with whom you hold significant differences, is not without its risks and rewards. But is it worth it? Let's find out.

---○---

Before You Arrive

Read the chapter and in fifty words or less, write about how it affects you.

_____

_____

_____

_____

Let the Conversation Begin

(Note: Be empowered to use as many or as few of these questions for your conversation time. Customize the use to your specific group.)

Describe your initial reaction, thoughts, and emotions to the chapter conversation topic centering around motivation for learning a language of healing. Remember, reactions can be positive or negative so be honest and authentic.

1. What is your main motivation or gain in learning a language of healing?

2. Which singular concept or aspect of this conversation was most impactful to you and why?

3. How would you describe your level of comfort or discomfort in assessing how to interact with someone "different"?

4. Identify one specific action that you see value in to pursue diverse relationships. Remember, if it is authentic to you, the action can be covert or overt.

Learning

Extrapolate two or three ideas, statements, or knowledge points from the conversation that are new to you, like the phrase, "What's in it for me?"

If the context and group size is conducive, pair up to discuss then share your partner's new ideas with the group or explain them back to your partner.

1. How would you describe your level of consciousness pertaining to your personal motivation?

2. Choose one idea in the chapter conversation that you want to adopt. What is it?

3. Which author's voice did you align with most?

4. Who will you need to reach out to for support? Or will you not require support?

5. Differentiate your thoughts prior to reading the chapter conversation with your thoughts post conversation.

6. What will be one positive result if you follow through?

———————————————◖———————————————

Action: What Will You Do Differently?

At the end of this chapter, the authors offered three possible actions to help you implement a strategy for change. At this part of the process, consider taking an opportunity to reflective journal through each of the action points. As in any good reflection exercise, take time to pause and thoughtfully turn the new information you have gained into intentional personal insight.

Crawl: *Take note of how often you mentally refer to "those people" when you're frustrated at someone's words or actions. Uncover the false stereotype behind it and find a better way to respond that won't marginalize them.*

Walk: *What assumptions do you make about others that inhibit you from finding value in relating to someone different?*

Run: *Identify three personal benefits for you in relating to someone who is different politically, socially, or religiously.*

o Which action point is a priority for you right now?

o How will you explain or elaborate on your personal reasons for embracing change?

o How much time will you give yourself to generate a plan?

Share

1. Who in your sphere of influence needs to hear this?

2. Going forward, what personal information pertaining to the "what's in it for me" mentality will you share with others to challenge their assumptions and/or conclusions?

3

Pardon Me, Your Tribe Is Showing

———————●———————

Do we want to live in a society where divergent tribes fight over who can gain the most advantage for themselves through legislation and public perception, or do we want to build a society that is fair for all, despite our differences?

If we choose the latter, we will be swimming upstream against a powerful current, not only of human instinct, but also of the commercial potential derived from fomenting the very adversity that's destroying us. Tribalism shows itself almost everywhere and the question that confronts us is whether we have the courage to recognize it and move beyond it.

Before You Arrive

After reading chapter three, take several minutes to ponder the following thoughts and questions:

1. When you finished reading this chapter, what was foremost on your mind? It can be an observation, a question, or a concern.

2. How has the talk of other people promoted fear in your own life about their intentions or motivations?

3. Recall one time when tribalism was a positive resource for you and one time when it proved to be a problem for you or someone you care about.

Let the Conversation Begin

(Note: Be empowered to use as many or as few of these questions for your conversation time. Customize the use to your specific group.)

Select one or two of the following questions to help you dive into the chapter on tribalism together. You may process these as an entire group or break into smaller groups to allow people more time to share.

1. How familiar were you with the ideas in this chapter before you read it?

   Very   Somewhat   So-so   Not at all

2. Do you think minority groups in a given context think more about tribal identities than people in majority groups? Why or why not?

3. What have you previously read or thought about tribalism? Where has it benefited you and where has it harmed you?

Learning

Pair up to discuss then share your partner's new ideas with the group or explain them back to your partner.

1. What two or three ideas or statements were new to you?

2. What in-groups do you identify with?

3. Identify the out-groups you wish you knew more about.

4. What value do you place on having a greater understanding of the concerns of your out-groups?

5. What fears will you have to face to get to know other people who aren't like you?

6. Think of one person in an out-group that you could get to know and understand better, without having to convince them of anything.

Action: What Will You Do Differently?

At the end of this chapter the authors offered three possible actions to help you implement a strategy for change. At this part of the process, consider taking an opportunity to reflective journal through each of the action points. As in any good reflection exercise, take time to pause and thoughtfully turn the new information you have gained into intentional personal insight.

Crawl: *Recognize when you deem someone in your out-group as "stupid" for not having the same views you do. Instead can you think of a good reason why they might hold those views?*

Walk: *Identify what in-groups you consider yourself a part of and what out-groups you tend to avoid. Can you see yourself learning more about an out-group?*

Run: *Invite a person in your out-group into a conversation with the intent of gaining understanding from their point of view.*

Identify *one* specific action you see value in pursuing from this chapter. You can choose from the list above or come up with your own. Remember, the action can be covert or overt as long as it is authentic to you.

o Elaborate on why you made this action a priority.

○ Is there an ideal context (work, church, home, community) for you to use the new information? What makes that an ideal place to begin?

○ How will you express your new action to others? Or will you?

○ Will you need support to help you implement this change? If so, who will you ask to support you?

Share

1. Who else in your sphere of influence could benefit from what you learned about tribalism?

2. Going forward, what personal information will you share with others to challenge their assumptions and/or conclusions about you?

3. The next time you are in a room where one of your "tribes" is making unfair judgments about an out-group, will you speak up?

4. What might you say or do to help people think outside the box of their own experience and see the situation the way someone with different experiences would?

4

The Symphony of Different

———————————◐———————————

There have been moments in history when those with differing agendas found the ability to work together toward a common goal. From politicians to movie studio execs, we've seen agendas set aside for peace, money, and sometimes both. Perhaps there is no better example in sports than the 1992 Olympic "Dream Team." The roster representing the United States featured sworn enemies Larry Bird, Magic Johnson, and Michael Jordan. Each player had already won several NBA championships by the time the '92 Olympics rolled around; they had met one another on the court multiple times with titles on the line. Larry Bird, the greatest trash-talker in history, had famously refused to even socialize with those who were not on his team.

Everything changed in 1992, as this trio took the court together at the Barcelona Olympic Games. Not only did they make history—winning every game by an average margin of nearly forty-four points—they did it by becoming consummate teammates. During their eight-game stretch, all three of them intentionally sought to lift the games of other players on the team, resulting in fewer personal scoring opportunities. Their choice, however, to work in concert with one another caused many sports journalists to refer to the "Dream Team" as the single greatest sports team ever assembled.

Their example epitomized the concept of team over individual, regardless of their differences. In the same way, if we can find a way to work together beyond our differences, we can accomplish some incredible things.

Before You Arrive

After reading chapter four, take several minutes to ponder the following thoughts and questions:

1. Think back to a time when being part of a team made a positive difference. Specifically, how was your experience enhanced?

2. Acquaint yourself with *relational trust* and *functional trust*. Can you think of incidents where each has been apparent in your life?

3. Can you remember a time when you were thrust into a team with people different from you? In what way did they differ?

Let the Conversation Begin

(Note: Be empowered to use as many or as few of these questions for your conversation time. Customize the use to your specific group.)

Break into groups of three or four and discuss the following:

1. Have you ever experienced differing degrees of judgment based on your level of relationship? Has the depth of a relationship ever dismantled your judgment?

2. Discuss how *like* often works as a collective: different voices working together to achieve a common purpose. Give examples from your own lives.

3. Have you found your degree of judgment to be based on your level of relationship? Give an example.

Learning

Think of a group of people who are not like you. List three things that you still have in common.

Learn to **PLAY** together.

o **P**urpose to contribute your individual best to the whole relationship of your orchestra, tribe, or society.

o **L**everage your current networks since you have a closer proximity. Symphony sections are very close to each other.

o **A**ccept the personal discomfort of being challenged to understand and appreciate something different.

o **Y**ield your heart and mind to the new sound and the composite beauty you will discover.

Action: What Will You Do Differently?

At the end of this chapter the authors offered three possible actions to help you implement a strategy for change. At this part of the process, consider taking an opportunity to reflective journal through each of the action points. As in any good reflection exercise, take time to pause and thoughtfully turn the new information you have gained into intentional personal insight.

Crawl: *When you share your thoughts with people who think differently from you, do not communicate as if your view is the most salient perspective. Think of yours as one of many.*

Walk: *Never assume you or anyone else can accurately guess someone else's motives. It is the easiest way to unjustly smear others, so you can dismiss them. Ask yourself how you'd hear people differently if you assumed their motives were honorable?*

Run: *Identify three examples this week where you could appreciate someone's insight or actions that you have previously dismissed because they are different from yours.*

Share

For some, "playing well with others" comes easy. For many of us, the thought of community spaces frightens us. Be intentional to spend time with those who complement your natural tendencies. You'll find that these people are often opposite to you. Seek out new friendships and new players in your personal symphony.

5

Staking Out the Common Ground

———————————————•———————————————

Many think they find common ground when they can convince enough people to agree with them so they can get their way. They view the world through polarized lenses, with each issue offering two opposing and mutually exclusive options—one right the other wrong. Of course, they think themselves on the side of right and look on those who disagree with disdain.

The common ground, however, is not where we all agree, but where we map out an environment in which we can discuss our differences with mutual respect and seek a solution that is fair to those differences. That's why our Founders established our nation not as a democracy but a Democratic Republic. Thomas Jefferson pointed out why: "A democracy is nothing more than mob rule, where 51 percent of the people may take away the rights of the other 49 percent."

The higher aspirations of our "more perfect union" is to find that common ground where the rights of all are respected and the liberty of all protected. Nowhere is that needed more than where we disagree on critical issues. That may be unthinkable in an age of polarizing politics, but that only makes it a nobler pursuit.

Before You Arrive

After reading chapter five, take several minutes to ponder the following thoughts and questions:

1. When you finished reading this chapter, what was foremost on your mind? It can be an observation, a question, or a concern.

2. How does this chapter define *common ground*? Is that how you saw it before reading this chapter?

3. When someone disagrees with your political or social views, how do you view them?

4. What fears do you have of people in our culture who don't look like you or think like you?

Let the Conversation Begin

(Note: Be empowered to use as many or as few of these questions for your conversation time. Customize the use to your specific group.)

1. Did the application of the founding ideals of your country include you?

2. In having a difficult or controversial conversation with someone, how would you want the other person to respond to you, especially when they disagree with you?

3. Think of the most polarizing person you know. Without identifying them or their relationship to you, find some words to describe how they make you feel.

4. Describe what a "reasonable person" looks like to you? What makes it safe for you to discuss controversial issues with someone?

5. Have you ever been in a decision-making group where one of the key stakeholders was omitted? What if that were you?

6. Does building the common ground as described in this chapter require us to agree on the issues? What does it require?

Learning

If the context is conducive, pair up to discuss then share your partner's new ideas with the group or explain them back to your partner.

1. Identify two or three ideas or concepts that were new to you.

2. How often do you come to conclusions about an issue without even considering how the opposing view thinks or feels? If not, ask yourself who you could approach to help you understand what's behind their thinking?

3. How much do you take into account the desire of others for the same freedoms you want for yourself?

4. How can a mutual respect for a "Liberty of Conscience" help us build respect for people we disagree with?

5. How would it change the public dialogue if we stopped fighting for our own preferences and started looking for a way to share our public spaces by being fair to the differences of every reasonable person represented at the table?

Action: What Will You Do Differently?

At the end of this chapter the authors offered three possible actions to help you implement a strategy for change. At this part of the process, consider taking an opportunity to reflective journal through each of the action points. As in any good reflection exercise, take time to pause and thoughtfully turn the new information you have gained into intentional personal insight.

Crawl: *Instead of dismissing others, thinking them less than you, find ways to ask for more information to help you understand them. Use phrases such as these: "What I hear you saying is..." This will help decrease your need to be defensive.*

Walk: *Take a long look at someone you tend to treat dismissively because of the way they look or think. How can you begin to reach out to them as a fellow human being?*

Run: *Think about how society is unfair to a minority person you know. What could you do to bring more equity to the person you know?*

o Which action point is a priority for you right now?

o Why would you want to make a change in this area for your own life?

◐ When will you take action on one of these points above and how will you do it?

Share

1. Who else in your sphere of influence needs to hear what you have learned in this discussion?

2. Going forward, what personal information will you share with others to challenge their assumptions and/ or conclusions about you?

3. In the future, before you start resolving an issue with any team of people, ask yourself who is missing from the room that should be represented? How can you suggest they be included?

SECTION 2

Five Practices of a Peacemaker

Speaking the language of healing isn't a matter of semantics alone; it's also a matter of developing your character. When we are more at peace with ourselves, we will not be threatened by those who have different perspectives or beliefs. In fact, they can add to our own experience and enrich it.

Then we can work for a more generous public square, wanting others to enjoy the same benefits of a free society that we want for ourselves.

Here are five practices you can cultivate in your own character that will enable you to speak the language of healing.

6

Being Comfortable in Your Own Skin

Mark Twain said, "The worst loneliness is to not be comfortable with yourself." Brené Brown seems to agree. "True belonging only happens when we present our authentic, imperfect selves to the world, our sense of belonging can never be greater than our level of self-acceptance." The art of self-acceptance—being comfortable in our skin—is a skill that requires the ability to adapt as we live life. Sadly, many never acquire the proper skills necessary to navigate. Well, maybe most don't. For those who are willing to make the investment in themselves, life becomes a richer and more rewarding experience.

Before You Arrive

Read the chapter and in fifty words or less, write about how it affects you.

_____

_____

_____

_____

Let the Conversation Begin

(Note: Be empowered to use as many or as few of these questions for your conversation time. Customize the use to your specific group.)

Describe your initial reaction, thoughts, and emotions to being comfortable in your own skin. Remember, reactions can be positive or negative so be honest and authentic.

1. How does being secure give you an advantage in learning a language of healing?

2. Can you recall a time that you felt different because of your skin?

3. Which one concept or aspect of this conversation was most impactful to you and why?

4. Why is skin color often a negative trigger?

5. Identify *one* specific action you think will be valuable as you pursue diverse relationships while possibly facing rejection. Remember, the action can be covert or overt—either is fine as long as it is authentic to you.

6. Elaborate on why you made this action a priority.

——————————————— ◐ ———————————————

Learning

Extrapolate two to three ideas, statements, or knowledge points from the conversation that are new to you.
If the context is conducive, pair up to discuss, then share your partner's new ideas with the group or explain them back to your partner.

1. How would you describe your level of personal insecurity ranging from totally unfamiliar to familiar with a new understanding?

2. Choose one idea in the chapter conversation that you want to adopt. What is it? Who will you need to support you in making this a reality?

3. Which author's voice did you align with most?

4. Differentiate your thoughts prior to reading the chapter conversation with your thoughts post conversation.

5. In what ways does your level of personal insecurity diminish your ability to build relationships, especially with people who differ?

Action: What Will You Do Differently?

At the end of this chapter the authors offered three possible actions to help you implement a strategy for change. At this part of the process, consider taking an opportunity to reflective journal through each of the action points. As in any good reflection exercise, take time to pause and thoughtfully turn the new information you have gained into intentional personal insight.

Crawl: *Think of a time when someone could have easily taken offense to a careless comment and chose not to. What did they say or do to disarm the situation?*

Walk: *What situations make you insecure? How can you effectively mitigate those feelings?*

Run: *Identify a person you perceive as being very comfortable in their own skin and connect with them in the next thirty days.*

○ Which action point is a priority for you right now?

○ How will you explain or elaborate your personal reasons for embracing change?

---○---

Share

1. Who in your sphere of influence needs to hear this?

2. Going forward, what personal information pertaining to the ability to conquer rejection will you share with others to challenge their assumptions and/or conclusions?

3. How will you explain to someone what you have done differently?

7

Cultivating Compassion

—◦—

Father Gregory Boyle, the author of the best-selling book Tattoos on the Heart, once said "Here is what we seek: a compassion that can stand in awe at what the poor have to carry rather than stand in judgment at how they carry it."

Even though his focus was the poor, it's easy to insert the word humanity into his thought. Compassion, although technically a noun, is at its core, an action word. Being moved without taking action is simply pity. Compassion will not allow us to feel and not act on behalf of others.

—◦—

Before You Arrive

After reading chapter seven, take several minutes to ponder the following thoughts and questions:

1. Remember a time in your life when you were shown genuine compassion. How did it make you feel? What thoughts or emotions did it evoke—positive or negative?

2. Consider the opposite effects of willful ignorance and proximity. Does one action open the door to compassion wider than the other?

3. Recall a time when acting as judge and jury reduced your level for compassion.

Let the Conversation Begin

(Note: Be empowered to use as many or as few of these questions for your conversation time. Customize the use to your specific group.)

Break into groups of three or four and discuss the following:

1. Do the concepts of compassion excite you? Does compassion scare you? Why?

2. What part does empathy—putting ourselves in someone else's shoes—play in living a life of compassion?

3. How do we start to develop a life of compassion?

4. Discuss the relationship between courage—doing things that scare us—and compassion. Why is it important to live a life of courageous compassion?

Learning

1. How familiar were you with the three levels of compassion: primary, secondary, and tertiary? Can you find examples that fit each level?

2. How does proximity help us develop compassion?

3. How does listening enhance our conversations to model compassion?

4. Pair up to discuss what it means to remove the judge's robe and to stand beside each one we meet as an advocate. How will this action change how you view those in the LGBTQ community?

Action: What Will You Do Differently?

At the end of this chapter the authors offered three possible actions to help you implement a strategy for change. At this part of the process, consider taking an opportunity to reflective journal through each of the action points. As in any good reflection exercise, take time to pause and thoughtfully turn the new information you have gained into intentional personal insight.

Crawl: *Learn to listen with compassion without invalidating the other person's position or feelings. Take note of how often you use words like always or never in talking about others. See if you can eliminate those words in such discourse.*

Walk: *In the next three days, look for one way to show a random act of compassion to another person. How does it make you feel about yourself?*

Run: *Model compassion by scheduling time with someone you can bless.*

Share

As you step into a more intentionally compassionate lifestyle, you will collect stories that can be shared with others. Humbly share those stories and help others see the value in compassion.

We are faced with the choice to be compassionate nearly every single day. Whether it's a stranger holding a sign on the corner, a young mother struggling with her children in a grocery store, or our spouse or children exhausting our patience, we can always find opportunities to practice compassion. Make it your practice to feel empathy for those around you.

8

Listen Up!

The Urban Dictionary defines listen up as something you say to people who have no idea what's going on. How often do we react to people around us without an understanding or appreciation for what is happening in their life? Everyone has a story. Some tell it eagerly. Some need it drawn out. But for many the pathway to healing begins with someone willing to listen to their story.

Several years ago, I was part of a local outreach to the homeless population. We would hand out chicken sandwiches to people on the street. I was surprised that so many people wanted to tell me how they ended up homeless. Many of them had made one bad decision that landed them on the streets— one moment with far-reaching consequences.

In our previous chapter, we focused on compassion. Listening to others—to hear and to acknowledge someone's story—is a critical component that will help express and grow our compassion. If you interpret someone else's words in your own framework, you have no idea what they are trying to say. You have to interpret it in theirs. Learning any language involves hearing as much as speaking. The good news is that listening is a skill we can all develop to make us more effective communicators and healers.

———————————————————○———————————————————

Before You Arrive

Read the chapter and, in fifty words or less, write about how it affects you.

_____

_____

_____

_____

_____

———————————————————○———————————————————

Let the Conversation Begin

(Note: Be empowered to use as many or as few of these questions for your conversation time. Customize the use to your specific group.)

Describe your initial reactions, thoughts, and emotions as they relate to listening to others. Remember, reactions can be positive or negative so be honest and authentic.

On a scale of 1 to 10, how would you rate your current ability to hear another person's narrative?

Which one concept or aspect of this conversation was most impactful to you and why?

Learning

Extrapolate two or three ideas, statements, or knowledge points from the conversation that are new to you.

*If the context is conducive, pair up to discuss. Share your partner's new ideas with the group or explain them back to your partner.

1. Do you listen to help others feel validated and heard? Or do you listen in a manner that makes others feel shut out?

2. How do you harness your personal filters in order to listen without defensiveness?

3. Which author's voice did you align with most?

4. In conversations, do you think you are a safe place for others to land? If yes, why? If not, why not?

5. Which conversations are easier for you to listen to?

Action: What Will You Do Differently?

At the end of this chapter the authors offered three possible actions to help you implement a strategy for change. At this part of the process, consider taking an opportunity to reflective journal through each of the action points. As in any good reflection exercise, take time to pause and thoughtfully turn the new information you have gained into intentional personal insight.

Crawl: *Listen to someone this week to understand them; not to solve their problem or rebut their conclusion. It is rarely necessary to add your thoughts to their story unless invited to do so. If you need more clarity, use these phrases:*
- *"Help me understand..."*
- *"Please explain..."*
- *"What's your experience with..."*
- *"What are your thoughts on..."*

Walk: *After conversations, journal why or why not you may have found it difficult to listen and understand what the person was trying to communicate.*

Run: *Practice. Practice. Practice.*

○ Which action point is a priority for you right now?

Share

1. Who in your sphere of influence needs to hear this?

2. How will you explain to someone why you are being more attentive?

9

From My Good to Our Good

———————————◦———————————

It's often not that hard to know what I think is good for me. We know our own needs well and have a sense of fairness built around our preferences. However, looking beyond my individual good to see what is best for others around me is something else altogether. Moving from my good, to all of our good, is a great test of maturity.

Individualism is a powerful reality when it challenges us to take care of ourselves and rise to whatever life our talents and diligence can take us. But when it means everyone grabs for their own, without regard to what is fair for all, it can be incredibly destructive.

What creates an environment that allows someone to shift from looking out for their own interests, to embracing a common good that ensures the same opportunities, protections, and freedoms for others that I want for myself?

———————————◦———————————

Before You Arrive

After reading chapter nine, take several minutes to ponder the following thoughts and questions:

1. When you finished reading this chapter, what was foremost on your mind? It can be an observation, a question, or a concern.

2. What cultures other than your own would you like to know more about so you won't feel uncertain about your actions when you're near them?

3. Name a group you've grown more comfortable with because you got to know some people in that group.

Let the Conversation Begin

(Note: Be empowered to use as many or as few of these questions for your conversation time. Customize the use to your specific group.)

1. React to this statement: "We belong to each other." What does that mean to you? How could you apply that in a meaningful way? Where do you think that sentiment is misused?

2. Why does our political machinery offer us what we want at someone else's expense, instead of appealing to fairness for all?

3. What challenges you to look beyond selfishness to sacrifice something meaningful for someone else?

4. How can generosity make up for the disadvantages of others?

Learning

*If the context is conducive, pair up to discuss then share your partner's new ideas with the group or explain them back to your partner.

1. Identify two or three ideas or concepts in this chapter that were new to you.

2. If you had more advantages than most in your formative years, how did that make you feel?

3. If you had fewer advantages than most in your formative years, how did that make you feel?

4. What experiences make you more aware of the needs of others?

5. Where have you encountered unfairness in your culture? Is there anything you could have done about it? Is there something someone else could have done?

―――――――――――――――○―――――――――――――――

Action: What Will You Do Differently?

At the end of this chapter the authors offered three possible actions to help you implement a strategy for change. At this part of the process, consider taking an opportunity to reflective journal through each of the action points. As in any good reflection exercise, take time to pause and thoughtfully turn the new information you have gained into intentional personal insight.

Crawl: *In conversations about different racial views, how do you inject denial, minimization, or victim-shaming into someone else's story and how do you feel it has been used against you? How can you avoid doing that in the future?*

Walk: *Examine how your racial views were shaped in your formative years. Summarize them and discuss with a friend how they affect you today.*

Run: *This week, intentionally defend someone different from you to someone who is like you.*

o Which action point is a priority for you right now?

o Why would you want to make a change in this area for your own life?

o When will you take action on one of these points above and how will you do it?

Share

1. Who else in your sphere of influence needs to hear what you have learned in this discussion?

2. Going forward, what personal information will you share with others to challenge their assumptions and/ or conclusions about you?

3. How can you humanize those people for whom you seem to have less empathy than might be appropriate?

10

Willing to be Disruptive

In a 2003 Harvard Business Review *article, writers Gary Hamel and Liisa Välikangas defined resilience as "a capacity to undergo deep change without or prior to a crisis." People with that kind of foresight are rare. Most people don't see the need for change until a crisis forces them into it.*

Sometimes crisis comes as a result of unforeseen circumstances, but they also result from someone who is willing to risk disrupting the status quo. Shawn Fanning created a disturbance in the entertainment industry with the first file-sharing application known as Napster in 2002. Former NFL player Colin Kaepernick disrupted our social awareness by kneeling for the National Anthem in 2016. Without those who are willing to cause disruption, we might very well still be living in the Stone Age.

Before You Arrive

After reading chapter nine, take several minutes to ponder the following thoughts and questions:

1. Can you recall a time when disruption offered a positive benefit for society?

2. Can you remember a disruption that had a negative impact?

3. What are the risks of disruption within a society?

Let the Conversation Begin

(Note: Be empowered to use as many or as few of these questions for your conversation time. Customize the use to your specific group.)

1. Are there instances where disruption becomes unwelcome or unnecessary?

2. Identify and discuss specific individuals who have disrupted our society. Here are some examples: Dr. Martin Luther King Jr., Colin Kaepernick, and President Trump. What was the impact of their disruption upon the culture?

3. Discuss the concept of courage leading to social disruption. Can you think of positive examples? Negative examples?

―――――――――――――――――◉―――――――――――――――――

Learning

1. Take a moment to identify and assess your personal history with societal disruption. Did it make you uncomfortable? Was the outcome positive and, in the end, worth it?

2. Think of a time when you were able to enhance the personal freedom of someone else. Was there a personal cost to you?

3. In the book, Arnita and her family made the conscious decision to attend a church that was culturally unlike how they had been raised. Are there ways that you can disrupt your own personal status quo? Take a moment to write down a few ideas.

―――――――――――――――――◉―――――――――――――――――

Action: What Will You Do Differently?

At the end of this chapter the authors offered three possible actions to help you implement a strategy for change. At this part of the process, consider taking an opportunity to reflective journal through each of the action points. As in any good reflection exercise, take time to pause and thoughtfully turn the new information you have gained into intentional personal insight.

Crawl: *Be careful not to use being a disrupter as an excuse to be a jerk by yelling, name-calling, and interrupting others in your conversations.*

Walk: *When you realize that people you know either mis-understand or are belittling the views of another, is it difficult for you to risk those relationships to help them learn something helpful? If so, why?*

Run: *Set aside a time to visit an unfamiliar place void of your normal crowd. Just sit there for fifteen to thirty minutes. If you dare, talk to someone different.*

Share

1. Find a friend or two to share in the journey of positive disruption. Be intentional in your actions, as well as your times together.

2. Identify an aspect of your life that has become stagnant. Find the courage to begin to make positive changes.

3. Reach out to someone not in your normal circle and begin to listen and engage with new purpose.

SECTION 3

Operating in Shared Space

We all have preferences of belief and action that we can freely live out in the privacy of our lives and our associations. However, a representative democracy asks us to cooperate in the shared spaces of our society, rather than co-opt them for one point of view over another.

Learning to operate generously in these shared spaces will allow us to build that "more perfect union," not because we all agree, but because we respect one another beyond our disagreements. None of our political parties, media, lobbyists, or political action committees help us fight for this shared space. It will take the generosity of ordinary citizens to build this space to enrich all of our lives.

11

Disarming the Binary Bomb

In 2018, More in Common *released a study called "The Hidden Tribes of America" that documented how most of our polarization is being fomented and funded by 6 percent of the population that they designated as the Progressive Activists and 27 percent of the population that they called the Traditional and Devoted Conservatives. Their amplification of our political issues has created a binary approach, where someone has to be completely right and the other has to be completely wrong.*

The good news is that the rest of the population, nearly two-thirds—termed the Exhausted Majority—are tired of the vitriol, reject the binary options offered by those on the extreme, and want a more civil discussion of the issues that get to more nuanced and effective solutions.

This is the place where the language of healing can be most effective. It will not deter those on the extremes, but it can give a language for the Exhausted Majority to find not only each other but also better options for the issues that confound us. We can disarm the binary bomb that politicians and media have been handing us for decades and invite the kind of conversations that will heal our divide rather than perpetuate it. To do that we will have to move beyond binary thinking and invite others to reject the contrived options the extremists use to turn on each other.

Before You Arrive

After reading chapter eleven, take several minutes to ponder the following thoughts and questions:

1. When you finished reading this chapter, what was foremost on your mind? It can be an observation, a question, or a concern.

2. Think of an issue that society presents to us in binary options, and see if you can come up with a range of related concerns that provide more options than just A and B.

3. Think of the last three people you conversed with who held different views than yours. Were you more engaged listening to them, or trying to prove them wrong?

Let the Conversation Begin

(Note: Be empowered to use as many or as few of these questions for your conversation time. Customize the use to your specific group.)

1. Where did this chapter make you think outside your box?

2. Name some public issues that are almost always presented as extreme binary options?

3. Pick one of those issues and discuss the nuanced issues behind those options that the media or politicians ignore?

4. How do binary options feed our inclination to judge right and wrong, instead of appreciating the different perspectives that are in our culture?

5. What is the "power of simultaneous"? Can you think of an example where your friends wouldn't allow you to hold two true things in tension, requiring you to embrace a simplified choice on one side or the other?

6. How can you expand your consideration of issues beyond binary choices and see a spectrum of possibilities you can use to negotiate with others?

7. Why do we need to beware of the conclusions of those who are profiting from polarization in our culture?

Learning

If the context is conducive, pair up to discuss then share your partner's new ideas with the group or explain them back to your partner.

1. Identify two or three ideas or concepts that were new to you.

2. Think of a recent example of someone giving you two options and you felt uncomfortable because you wondered what options they were intentionally leaving out to manipulate your response?

3. Discuss the difference between private activities and navigating shared space with people in a democratic republic who are very different from us? How can we do better at the latter?

4. Why is moving beyond binary thinking critical to resolve some of the issues that confront our culture?

Action: What Will You Do Differently?

At the end of this chapter the authors offered three possible actions to help you implement a strategy for change. At this part of the process, consider taking an opportunity to reflective journal through each of the action points. As in any good reflection exercise, take time to pause and thoughtfully turn the new information you have gained into intentional personal insight.

Crawl: *When you are with people who differ from you, salt your conversation with questions like, "What do you think about... ?" or "Your perspective is an interesting way of looking at that. Have you also considered...?" and see what happens.*

Walk: *Describe a current situation you're involved in that is filled with seemingly unresolvable conflict. What other options are you not considering?*

Run: *Identify by name a person you can bring into a difficult conversation who will have a different perspective. Contact them to discuss specifics.*

o Which action point is a priority for you right now?

o For your own life, why would you want to make a change in this area?

o When will you take action on one of these points and how will you do it?

Share

1. Who else in your sphere of influence needs to hear what you have learned in this discussion?

2. Going forward, what personal information will you share with others to challenge their assumptions and/ or conclusions about you?

3. This week, see how often you catch yourself trapped in a binary framework and then intentionally expand your perspective to consider other options?

4. When you are faced with a binary thinker, what question or questions might you ask to help them think beyond their narrow frame of reference without attacking them?

12

Bust Up Your Bias

———————————————•———————————————

Bias is a prejudice in favor of or against one thing, person, or group compared to another, usually in a way considered to be unfair. The great poet T. S. Eliot once said, "We can at least try to understand our own motives, passions, and prejudices, so as to be conscious of what we are doing when we appeal to those of others. This is very difficult, because our own prejudice and emotional bias always seems to us so rational." Bias influences almost every human interaction we have, and it is most insidious when we're least aware of it. Identifying our biases and disarming them is a critical component to employing the language of healing.

Before You Arrive

Read the chapter and, in fifty words or less, write about how it affects you.

———————————————————————————————————

———————————————————————————————————

———————————————————————————————————

———————————————————————————————————

Let the Conversation Begin

(Note: Be empowered to use as many or as few of these questions for your conversation time. Customize the use to your specific group.)

1. Describe your initial reaction, thoughts, and emotions to this statement: "Everyone has bias." Remember, reactions can be positive or negative so be honest and authentic.

2. What is your main motivation for identifying areas in which you have a strong negative bias?

3. Which one concept or aspect of this conversation was most impactful to you and why?

4. How do your personal biases affect your decisions and behavior toward others, especially those who are different?

5. Identify *one* specific action you see value in knowing your biases. Remember, the action can be covert or overt if it is authentic to you.

Learning

Extrapolate two or three ideas, statements, or knowledge points from the conversation that are new to you.

*If the context is conducive, pair up to discuss then share your partner's new ideas with the group or explain them back to your partner.

1. Choose one idea in the chapter conversation that you want to adopt. What is it?

2. Which author's voice did you align with most?

3. Differentiate your thoughts prior to reading the chapter conversation with your thoughts post conversation.

4. Exposure reduces negative bias. Who can you connect with to help you reduce yours?

Action: What Will You Do Differently?

At the end of this chapter the authors offered three possible actions to help you implement a strategy for change. At this part of the process, consider taking an opportunity to reflective journal through each of the action points. As in any good reflection exercise, take time to pause and thoughtfully turn the new information you have gained into intentional personal insight.

Crawl: *Understand that language has bias and see if you can remove language that is full of false assumptions and perpetuates stereotypes involving religion, sex, politics, gender, and race. For example, you would not say, "All black men..." "All Muslim women..." All Evangelical Christians..." All white women..." "All Mexican men..."*

Walk: *Out of the three biases in our discussion—implicit bias, truth bias, or confirmation bias—which one of these most inhibits your ability to relate to people who are different?*

Run: *Identify an area where you know you have bias and an area that you suffer from bias against you. The next time you are in a conversation that makes you uncomfortable, identify your bias..*

◑ Which action point is a priority for you right now?

———————————◐———————————

Share

Who in your sphere of influence needs to hear this?

Going forward, what personal information pertaining to bias and its effects will you share with others to challenge their assumptions and/or conclusions?

13

Sharing the Table

———————————————◦———————————————

"All great change in America begins at the dinner table."
—President Ronald Reagan

Whether we're sharing food or sharing thought, the table has become a symbol of inclusion. In families, we learn to communicate and interact around the shared experience of sitting at the table. In business, a seat at the table is the equivalent of being heard. For many, the table is the first place where we learn our value—or lack thereof.

Healing or wounding—it can all be found at the table.

———————————————◦———————————————

Before You Arrive

After reading chapter thirteen, take several minutes to ponder the following thoughts and questions:

1. Think back to a time when you were excluded. How did that make you feel?

2. What does it mean to be a catalyst for change?

3. Recall a time when you shared your power with someone. How did that make you feel?

Let the Conversation Begin

(Note: Be empowered to use as many or as few of these questions for your conversation time. Customize the use to your specific group.)

Break into groups of three or four and discuss the following:

1. Discuss what it means to truly share the table with those who are different. Does the concept excite or scare you? Why?

2. Is change possible without being intentional? What are some ways that we can be intentional about inviting others to the table?

3. What does it mean to you to be a catalyst for change?

4. Discuss the benefits of relationships outside of those who are like us.

Learning

1. What effect does fear have on sharing the table with others?

2. If tolerance is considered a virtue, why do people often have issues with simply being tolerated?

3. How can this change the way you work with those who hold to a different faith than you, or claim none at all?

4. How might this affect the way you work with people in the LGBTQ Community?

5. How does listening enhance our conversations to model compassion?

Action: What Will You Do Differently?

At the end of this chapter the authors offered three possible actions to help you implement a strategy for change. At this part of the process, consider taking an opportunity to reflective journal through each of the action points. As in any good reflection exercise, take time to pause and thoughtfully turn the new information you have gained into intentional personal insight.

Crawl: *When you extend an invitation for someone different to join you at the table, make it personal and ensure that your tone and nonverbal cues are welcoming and sincere.*

Walk: *Within your circle of influence, how do you feel about challenging your own comfort zone and being a catalyst to invite difference to the table?*

Run: *Be an advocate for inclusion within the power structures you encounter. Inclusion welcomes diverse perspectives and thought and not just obvious difference like race and gender.*

Share

Begin to be intentional as you include others. Always recognize the difference between someone being welcome versus being intentionally invited. Once your intent lines up with inclusiveness, be sure that your actions line up, as well.

14

Friendly Fire

———————————— ○ ————————————

"When a man is hit by friendly fire, his blood pressure lowers and his morale sinks. I have been hit by friendly fire in my heart. Sighs spill from my body instead of blood." —Hideo Kojima There's an old saying that simply says, "Friendly fire isn't." Those words reflect the reality of wounds that are inflicted by those closest to us. And there's very little about it that's friendly, even though it's often accompanied by smiles or even good intentions. The truth is this: Pain is always deeper when it comes from those we know, love, and respect.

———————————— ○ ————————————

Before You Arrive

Read the chapter and, in fifty words or less, write about how it affects you.

_____

_____

_____

_____

Let the Conversation Begin

(Note: Be empowered to use as many or as few of these questions for your conversation time. Customize the use to your specific group.)

1. Describe your initial reaction, thoughts, and emotions to the topic of friendly fire. Remember, reactions can be positive or negative so be honest and authentic.

2. Which one concept or aspect of this conversation was most impactful to you and why?

3. How would you describe your level of comfort or discomfort in assessing how you interact with someone "different"?

4. Identify *one* specific word choice you see value in monitoring. Remember, this can be covert or overt if it is authentic to you.

Learning

Extrapolate two or three ideas, statements, or knowledge points from the conversation that are new to you.

*If the context is conducive, pair up to discuss then share

your partner's new ideas with the group or explain them back to your partner.

1. How would you describe your level of consciousness around friendly fire ranging from totally unfamiliar to familiar with a new understanding?

2. Which author's voice did you align with most?

3. Differentiate your thoughts prior to reading the chapter conversation with your thoughts post conversation.

Action: What Will You Do Differently?

At the end of this chapter the authors offered three possible actions to help you implement a strategy for change. At this part of the process, consider taking an opportunity to reflective journal through each of the action points. As in any good reflection exercise, take time to pause and thoughtfully turn the new information you have gained into intentional personal insight.

Crawl: *When you're concerned that something you are about to say could be taken wrongly, be honest about your concern as a way to open the door. "Please let me know if I'm saying something inappropriate here, but..."*

Walk: *Write about an instance where you were the instigator of friendly fire toward someone else. What impact did your actions have?*

Run: *Begin to intentionally monitor the sensitivity of your language when you are with people who are racially, culturally, or religiously different from you.*

   ○   Which action point is a priority for you right now?

Share

Who in your sphere of influence needs to hear this?

Going forward, what personal information pertaining to friendly fire will you share with others to challenge their assumptions and/or conclusions?

How will you explain to someone what you have done differently?

15

Custodians of a Common Good

———————————————— ◖ ————————————————

We have arrived at the last chapter. We hope that we have ignited your desire to speak a language of healing wherever you interact with others that look or think differently than you do. If that's all this book does, we will consider it a success.

However, to change the broader conversation in a world tormented by polarizing rhetoric, we hope to inspire a growing number of people to not only speak a language of healing, but also to become custodians of a common good. Of course, we will all look out for our own good and possibly the good of others we consider "our people." But for our society to function effectively, we need a growing number of people to also care about the common good—what is best for all others in our community.

Often our personal good and the common good are in conflict. That's especially true for those in the majority. Every one of us would want to maximize our freedom and opportunity. That can be done, of course, at the expense of the freedom and opportunity for others. As challenging as it might be, the common good seeks to build a society where freedom and opportunity are equal for all of us.

Before You Arrive

After reading chapter fifteen, take several minutes to ponder the following thoughts and questions:

1. When you finished reading this chapter, what was foremost on your mind? It can be an observation, a question, or a concern.

2. Think of the last conflict you were involved in with a group of people. Were they looking to be fair to all, or was the stronger group trying to force their way? How might that discussion have been different if people were working to be fair to everyone involved?

3. Think about the rights in your culture that mean the most to you. For you to secure that right, what responsibility does it require you to extend to others so we can all enjoy it?

Let the Conversation Begin

(Note: Be empowered to use as many or as few of these questions for your conversation time. Customize the use to your specific group.)

1. How would you describe your level of comfort or discomfort with this chapter?

2. What are some concrete ways you can begin to live more generously in this polarized world?

3. Read this statement: "You best protect your civil rights by protecting the rights of those with whom you disagree." Agree or disagree?

4. Do you consider that your racial make-up afforded you more privileges or challenges where you grew up? Describe some of them.

5. If you've expressed concerns about disadvantages you have, do you consider that you've been heard or been ignored?

Learning

*If the context is conducive, pair up to discuss then share your partner's new ideas with the group, or explain them back to your partner.

1. Identify two or three ideas or concepts that were new to you.

2. Describe the power of an environment of collaboration over building coalitions with like-minded people.

3. If you've been in a collaborative environment where everyone was working hard to take all people into consideration, describe that experience.

4. What do you think are important factors to facilitate an environment that can collaborate toward a mutually beneficial solution?

5. What's the best way for you to see the world from someone else's point of view? Note that you might not truly appreciate this yet.

6. What does it mean to you now to be a custodian of a common good? What will it allow you to do differently?

------------------◐------------------

Action: What Will You Do Differently?

At the end of this chapter, the authors offered three possible actions to help you implement a strategy for change. At this part of the process, consider taking an opportunity to reflective journal through each of the action points. As in any good reflection exercise, take time to pause and thoughtfully turn the new information you have gained into intentional personal insight.

Crawl: *According to* Harvard Business Review, *many times in situations needing innovation and creativity, the phrase, "How might we . . . ?" is crucial. It is inclusive and open language allowing many options to be considered for a win-win situation. Use it often when collaborating with people who differ.*

Walk: *Where can you be a voice for a common good that rises above your own personal preferences?*

Run: *Find one person who is disadvantaged and do something to open access for them in a way they can't do for themselves.*

o Which action point is a priority for you right now?

o Why would you want to make a change in this area for your own life?

o When will you take action on one of these points above and how will you do it?

Share

1. Who else in your sphere of influence needs to hear what you have learned in this discussion?

2. Going forward, what personal information will you share with others to challenge their assumptions and/or conclusions about you?

3. How will the content of this book shape the next conversation or engagement you have about political, sexual, religious, or racial issues?

Appendix

1

Facilitation Tips

———————————◦———————————

Some of our readers have expressed an interest in taking this information to others in a small group format, but they may not feel adequately skilled in facilitating a conversation.

Facilitating conversation in groups is a skill that can take a while to master, but we are sharing a few tips from past experiences. Your commitment to your group matters! Life change and personal transformation happen when we are in smaller contexts, dialoguing, and learning from one another. We grow whenever we try to understand other perspectives and experiences and practice active listening.

A. Determine Group Type: Special Interest, five to ten people. This group may be found in various contexts, both personal and professional.

B. Setting Common Ground Rules/Expectations:

   1. Dignity and respect are prerequisites

   2. Use a compassionate and empathic tone

3. Mutual appreciation is necessary (listen to each other)

4. Understand that agreement is *not* the goal in these conversations

5. Safeguard vulnerability as people share what they are learning; refrain from exploiting and mocking them

6. Extra patience is required for these conversations

C. Conversation Management

1. Honor the individual voice and contribution by letting people have their own observations, conclusions, awareness, and understanding.

2. Prioritize the Group. There is no need to convince others of right or wrong. Agreement is not the goal of our conversation; dialogue and discourse are. Structured learning, as in teaching, is not needed here. Remember, participants are evaluating and connecting what the authors discuss to their own experiences. They are making their own conclusions about new ideas. The key here is to resist controlling the group so that discovery happens through the conversations.

3. We highly recommend that you choose specific instances, stories, or aspects of the literal conversation in the book and focus there. Use what the authors

have written as much as possible. Being comfortable enough to engage in these conversations will be an evolving process.

4. Listen attentively without offering advice unless it is solicited. Be sure to validate diverse perspectives.

5. Say what you see as a talking prompt:

   o   I notice...

   o   It appears...

   o   It seems like...

6. Use a polling question to prompt conversation: "How many of you..."

7. Use a round robin technique, in which everyone who wants to takes a turn to answer or share. Give them a ninety second time limit.

8. To engage the group, allot part of the conversation time for people to ask questions to the group, especially if there is a question that is content-related to the book.

Appendix

2

Team-Building Exercises

———————————— ◐ ————————————

For those groups with the intention to journey through the entirety of this discussion guide, we want to offer a few ice-breakers and team-building activities that may help your group form initial connections with one another and the material to come.

A Picture Speaks a Thousand Words

A. Objective: This is a fun activity that can help break the ice for either a newly formed group or a group that is familiar with one another. This is a noninvasive activity that will allow each member to creatively share what images mean to them with regard to a specific topic, such as religion or politics.

Instructions for the Facilitator

1. Ask each member of the group to bring one to five images that represent a certain subject to them. (You can pick one specific topic and have them bring in one

photo or image, or you can give them a list of topics
and have them bring in a picture or image for each.)

2. At the beginning of the meeting, ask each person to
   share their picture and then give a one- to two-minute
   explanation about why their image is impactful to them.

3. After all the members have gone, open up the group
   to a conversation about what they observed. Possible
   debrief questions are below.

   ☉ Were there any themes?

   ☉ What was the most unique image someone
     brought in?

   ☉ What there an image that you felt was a misrepre-
     sentation of the topic?

If I Were a Movie Clip!

A. Objective: This is a fun way to allow each member to
   express a little bit about themselves.

B. Instructions for the Facilitator

   1. Ask each member to bring in a short clip from a
      movie or television show.

      ☉ This movie clip can either be a representation of
        who they are, or it can be an impactful example of
        a specific subject matter.

○ Example: Have them bring in a movie clip that is a representation of someone overcoming a significant struggle or trial.

2. Have each member give a brief explanation of why they chose that clip.

3. After all the clips have been shown, debrief with the group about what they observed about what the group members brought to share.

The Bias Quiz

A. Objective: To provide each of the group members a brief look at potential biases they may have. Taking the quiz as a group will allow the group as a whole to observe the different reactions and experiences each member has when taking the quiz.

B. Instructions for the Facilitator: Choose an online quiz that focuses on a specific bias that you want the group to discuss.

1. Examples
   ○ Gender Bias, Racial Bias, Age Bias
   ○ https://implicit.harvard.edu/implicit/selectatest.html

(The above link has several different quizzes created by Harvard University to test for biases.)

2. Have the group take the test together on their phone, tablet, or laptop and save their results.

3. Observe how each of the group members reacts to the different questions.

4. Once everyone has taken the quiz, debrief the results and the experience as an entire group.

About the Authors

Wayne Jacobsen

Wayne travels the world as an author and speaker on themes of spiritual intimacy and relational community, especially where people are in crisis. Some of his popular books include *He Loves Me*, *Finding Church*, and *A Man Like No Other*. He was also a coauthor and publisher of *The Shack*. The words *self-effacing* and *best-selling author* aren't often used together, but Wayne's insight and humor have opened doors around the world whether it means resolving religious–liberty conflicts in public education, helping starving tribes in Kenya build a viable economy, or helping people find a vibrant spiritual life.

A former pastor, Wayne now hosts Lifestream.org, which provides resources for spiritual growth, and a podcast at TheGodJourney.com to encourage people thinking outside the box of organized religion. Both have inspired countless people to a more vibrant faith and a greater understanding of living in the church Jesus is building in the world. He lives in Southern California with Sara, his wife of forty-four years, where they both enjoy their adult children and grandchildren.

Arnita Willis Taylor

Wise, practical, resourceful, and fun, Arnita relates to diverse people and helps them maximize their potential. She has an inspiring way of equipping people as a leader, minister, mentor, and coach. She is known for her gregarious personality and warm hospitality to guests in her home.

From Murfreesboro, Tennessee, Arnita graduated from the University of Tennessee-Knoxville with a Bachelor of Arts degree in Medical Technology and earned her Master of Science in Leadership from Walden University. Her professional background runs from clinical laboratory science to small groups pastoral ministry.

As the founder of EIGHT Leadership Development Group, Arnita serves leaders by assisting individuals, teams, and organizations. She is a passionate communicator who helps enrich and empower others, and because she intentionally places herself in diversified settings she regularly teaches across racial, denominational, and gender lines.

At home in Keller, Texas, she is the wife of thirty-one years to Michael and the proud and grateful mother of two sons, Evan and Nolan.

Robert L. "Bob" Prater

Bob Prater is a lover of God and also a lover of—and advocate for—people. With a background in business, media, and ministry, he is half of the podcast *A Christian & A Muslim Walk into a Studio* alongside American-Muslim leader, Emad Meerza. He spent several years in full-time ministry as both a pastor and an administrator.

He has started businesses as diverse as developing and producing for television to selling whatever he can find online, and he has been in the top 3 percent of online sellers in the world. Bob married his high school sweetheart, Danette, in Eugene, Oregon, more than forty years go. As the dad to three daughters and three sons-in-law, and the grandpa to ten grandchildren, he leads a small army as Santa each year to the forgotten and abandoned places where the poorest reside. He also functions as an "Elder at Large," helping people connect dots in his hometown of Bakersfield, California.